Balconies &

Roof Gardens

This book is dedicated to my husband Chris

I would like to thank Stephen Crisp who has been a source of inspiration and John Glover for his continuing support and encouragement.

Balconies &
Roof Gardens

*Themed Ideas
for Small Scale
Gardening*

Jenny Hendy

Contents

A Room

with a view

BALCONIES AND ROOF TOPS may be counted amongst the most bizarre and formidable sites in which to garden. But despite presenting a significant challenge from the horticultural point of view, they can also be most rewarding for a number of reasons.

The first and most obvious is the possibility of creating a leafy haven from which to sit and take in the view. In reality there may not be that much to admire, but you certainly get a different perspective on the world from such a vantage point. Secondly, the high-rise gardener is freed from much of the less exciting aspects

of plant culture such as mowing lawns, digging borders and weeding, although there is

still watering to be done. Divorced from reality, high up in your eyrie, you may also

feel free to indulge yourself, to ignore convention and

create a garden entirely for your own pleasure. This

book will certainly give you plenty of food for thought.

And finally, there is the question of exploiting the

available space and turning it into extra living

accommodation. The concept of the outdoor room is well

established and doesn't just have relevance in warmer

climes. Even when it is too cold to be outdoors, just the

knowledge that you could step into the garden if you

wanted to can make the space feel larger and less

restricted, and who could deny the attraction of being

able to look out on to flowers and foliage as opposed to bricks and mortar?

I hope that this book will be used as an inspirational guide by anyone

seeking either to create a balcony or roof garden from scratch or to improve their existing plot. However, the ideas and practical information presented here can also be

used by owners of tiny backyards, terraces, patios and courtyards at ground level and

This modern roof terrace has been transformed into a cheerful spot for dining alfresco. It is surrounded by productive as well as ornamental plants..

by anyone interested in creating a strong theme or look for their garden. A total of

seventeen different gardening styles are explored and specific design pointers given

concerning various topics such as architectural detailing, wall decoration, flooring,

furniture, lighting, containers and planting. The information is not presented as a blue-print for your garden, but rather as a way of approaching and developing a particular theme.

The text is richly illustrated throughout with photographs from around the world which have been selected to help you to visualize the ideas in each chapter. When you have read through the style guide, it would be well worth going back to the sections that most appeal to study the images in more detail because they contain a great deal of additional information.

In the second part of the book, 'Practical Considerations', you will find information on how to deal with the specific problems associated with making a garden on a balcony or roof, beginning with safety aspects and considerations of weight. There are details on how to create the right environment for plants and people and how to overcome the limitations of space. A major part covers all you need to know for successful container gardening including ways to ensure that the garden has colour and interest all the year round. And finally, there is a wealth of hints and tips on furnishing your garden and creating various features and focal points.

left:
So often it's the simple ideas that are the most effective! Bougainvillea is the star attraction of this elegant Greek balcony.

right:
Where there is a will...! This garden is literally built on the roof and, despite the apparent drawbacks of the site, the owners have managed to grow plants of amazing diversity.

Urban

retreat

SITTING WITHIN THE enclosure of a secluded garden you begin to forget the world outside. Gardens are a haven from work and traffic and the general hustle and bustle of urban life. Foliage softens and camouflages brickwork and masonry, filtering out noise and pollution, and the many shades of green have a soothing effect on the eye. Plants also attract wildlife – birds, buzzing insect life and butterflies, bringing us closer to nature. So how do you go about creating your own little piece of Eden when your balcony or roof space seems too tiny to bother with

left:
Golden hop clothes this arbour creating a secluded place to sit and enjoy the garden.

right:
This roof terrace is a veritable oasis of flower and foliage, including many sun-loving Mediterranean varieties which are ideal for exposed sites like this.

or has uninspiring, even depressing views?

The first task is to block out what you don't want to see and create a background which provides shelter for you and the plants. You won't necessarily need a high barrier or trellis screen as protection around a seating area – it may simply be a case of placing planted troughs along the top of a parapet, or fixing flower pots to balcony railings. Neither of these methods takes up valuable floor space. Partial screens are often more successful than solid barriers since they allow light to filter through and reduce the speed and turbulence of wind. Floor troughs planted

Containers planted with daffodils, hyacinths, tulips and forsythia bring a splash of colour to this charming town garden which has a strong background of evergreens for year-round interest. One of the advantages of gardening in containers is that once the various displays have finished, the pots and troughs can be moved to less prominent positions. Notice the planters ranged along the top of the parapet which help to provide privacy and shelter.

with shrubs and climbers with trellis attached along the back are an ideal solution.

The next step is to soften or camouflage brickwork and rendering. One method is to clad walls with trellis panels attached to battens. Pick a light and cheerful shade to give the garden a lift. You can leave the trellis plain or use it as support for climbers and wall shrubs or to hang flower-filled pots. If you don't want to cover up brickwork with wooden or plastic trellis support, you can make an almost invisible framework for plants using galvanised or plastic-coated wire stretched horizontally between vine eyes at 18 in (45 cm) intervals. In order to climb easily,

plants like clematis and jasmine also need a series of close-spaced vertical wires. Self-clingers such as ivy, *Hydrangea anomala petiolaris* and *Parthenocissus henryana* do require some initial support before they will climb independently. One way to do this is to fix the shoots in direct contact with the wall using plastic clips which are nailed in place.

The type of flooring will also influence the feel of the garden. Small paviours or slabs with mottled colouring and a textured surface have a soft appearance, and wooden decking and paviours both produce a more natural feel.

A screen of textured glass panels provides privacy but at the same time lets in light. It is largely obscured by a tiered arrangement of potted plants which creates a wall of colour.

far left:

Fence panels smothered in climbers create a secluded dining area. The simple white furniture and white-washed brickwork give the garden a Mediterranean feel and pots and troughs overflowing with plants soften the paving.

Overhead structures such as arches and pergolas give the garden space a room-like quality and also help with privacy. Alternatively, create your own secluded place to get away from it all by erecting an arbour over a seat and covering it with trellis screens, climbers and shrubs.

left:

A sunny Mediterranean-blue has been used to link both decking and furniture with the water which is separated from the garden by a strong rope line. Date palm and Cordyline add a sub-tropical feel.

On the
waterfront

EVEN IF YOU ONLY HAVE a glimpse of water, you can create a stronger visual link with it and enhance the view by reflecting marine colours and materials in the design and planting of your balcony or roof garden. Keep the lines simple and try to leave as much open space as possible to capture the feel of being out on the open water.

Most of us have a vivid mental picture of the seaside which can be drawn on for inspiration. Colour is an important starting point and a way of instantly transforming the existing hard landscape. Stain woodwork and paint railings in greys, blues, greens and white and follow this scheme through with silver and grey foliage, blue, mauve and white flowers. If you are by the sea, choose wind and salt-resistant plants. Hebes and herbs such as lavender, hyssop, rosemary and *Santolina* are ideal. For foliage contrast, try the silver-grey *Senecio* 'Sunshine' (now *Brachyglottis*), dwarf-growing *Pinus mugo* 'Mops' and sword-shaped leaves of phormiums and yuccas. Although wind can be a problem by the sea, one of the great advantages for the gardener of being close to a large body of water is that winter

temperatures are often slightly higher than in surrounding areas and may even be mild enough to grow frost-tender plants all year round.

Timber is often associated with the seaside in the form of beach huts, piers, boardwalks and sea defences. Decking makes an attractive, lightweight floor covering for balconies and roof gardens and you can also use horizontal wooden laths as screening or to cover the sides of large planters, built-in seats and storage units.

left:

The circular chair, resembling a piece of modern art, makes a striking contrast with the sword-shaped leaves of the agave. A stone bowl planted with succulents completes this simple picture.

For seating, why not use deck chairs or cover soft furnishings with traditional broad striped canvas. Use pebbles for mulching planters and groups of large cobbles for floor decoration. Stencils with seashells, starfish and other seaside motifs can be used to decorate woodwork, decking, and even fabric provided you select the appropriate paint. Protect decorative paintwork on wood and walls with several coats of clear exterior grade varnish.

To really make a feature of a bare wall, consider making bold mosaics by setting shells into soft cement rendering. Ask your local fishmonger to let you have any discarded scallop and cockle shells. Other innovative ideas for setting the scene include

above:

This garden has an unrivalled view of the river Thames and its famous landmark. An abstract sculpture of driftwood is perfectly in keeping with the modern design and architectural planting.

Bleached wood is a prominent material in this balcony's construction and gives it the feel of a beach hut. The blue and white furnishings and large container-grown palm help to strengthen that image.

using wave-sculpted pieces of driftwood, coloured glass fishing floats or a draped fishermen's net as a wall hanging.

There are a number of other visual devices which can be used to suggest a link with the sea such as incorporating elements associated with sailing ships or luxury ocean-going liners. Plain or varnished wooden decking is an obvious choice but also consider sweeping canvas awnings or screening panels lashed with rope. For the sailing ship motif decorate the 'deck' with a large rope coil, or have some fun and fly a flag from fake rigging. Suspend a hammock or make furniture from converted oak barrels. Use nautical motifs to decorate wooden furniture and built-in planters, e.g. rope knots and anchors.

Alternatively, on a more mythological note, why not paint a figure of Neptune or a sea serpent on a wall! If you are feeling less ambitious, try a stencilled border of stylized waves or leaping dolphins. The liner-look is more sophisticated, with brass fittings, thirties-style wooden deck loungers and stylish planters containing large architectural foliage plants such as the hardy palm *Trachycarpus fortunei* or *Cordyline australis*.

Sweeping sun shades like sails in the wind protect this stylish seating area which overlooks the coast. Decoration is kept to a minimum, reflecting the simplicity of the water's surface.

Romantic
appeal

left:

An elegant metal plant stand filled with lacecap hydrangeas makes an eye-catching focal point. Notice the line of clipped box globes in delightful striped pots beneath.

ROMANTIC GARDENS take us back to a more genteel era when chivalry was well and truly alive and young lovers would hold moonlight trysts beneath a scented bower of honeysuckle and rose. These gardens have a mysterious, almost magical air. To rekindle that atmosphere, it is essential to blur the boundaries and create a sense of enclosure. Trellis screens may have to be high and smothered with climbers to blot out any reference to the twentieth century.

You may be lucky enough to live in a building which has plenty of period detail, but it is more likely that you will have to import some of the decorations from

below:

Cool white flowers frame this water feature with a mythological wall mask. Old metal watering cans have been turned into imaginative ornaments.

elsewhere. A neo-Classical urn or statuette half hidden by lush foliage would pique the curiosity of a visitor. Water features are similarly enchanting – make the most of a shady corner by turning it into a secret grotto with water gently trickling from a wall

mask into a small fern-edged pool.

If you are sufficiently determined you could create a garden which looks as though it has been lost for years, gradually re-claimed by nature and only recently discovered. To do this, the planting should be exuberant and overflowing, with climbers festooning archways and pergolas with abandon. Soften the hard landscaping by deliberately sowing or planting the cracks in paving and steps with creeping colonisers such as the dainty daisy-flowered *Erigeron karvinskianus*, sweet white alyssum, double-flowered chamomile, alpine campanulas or lemon-scented thymes. Age new pots, planters and ornaments before putting them in position and try to find genuinely antique garden fixtures, regardless of how battered they have become over time. A certain amount of dilapidation will help to strengthen the illusion.

left:

A classical figure gazes down from on high. Rose-covered trellis panels and the white-washed wall screen the garden from the outside world and elegant wirework chairs make a strong decorative statement.

right:

This modern garden has been planted in a romantic style. Diamond trellis covers the walls and supports old-fashioned rambler roses; wisteria softens the railings and a large pot of Lilium regale *forms the centrepiece.*

Colour plays a significant role in romantic scene setting. White brings a cool elegance and purity. Against an all-white backdrop, create a pretty planting effect with white, cream, blush pink and lavender blue flowers, white-variegated and silver foliage. When choosing plants, try to include as many as possible with aromatic foliage or scented flowers. Remember, this is a garden to excite all the senses! The following plants release intoxicating perfumes – *Philadelphus*, *Osmanthus*, *Choisya*, *Buddleja davidii*, roses, jasmine, *Trachelospermum jasminoides*, hyacinth, lilies, double-flowered stocks, old-fashioned pinks, *Nicotiana sylvestris*, and mignonette. A richer, moodier and more sensuous scheme could be created using flowers and foliage in deep velvet reds and dusky purples highlighted by silver and grey leaved plants.

In the romantic garden, try to make the most of sculpted flowers of great

beauty, such as the large flowered bearded iris, the arum lily and the foxglove, combining them with plants with diaphanous foliage, for example bronze fennel (*Foeniculum vulgare* 'Purpureum'), and Artemisia 'Powis Castle'.

left:
A number of intimate seating areas have been created in this large roof garden using trellis screens and masses of potted plants including the golden Gleditsia triacanthos *'Sunburst', Japanese maples, smoke bush (*Cotinus*) and climbing roses.*

This tiny backyard with its pink and white colour scheme has been transformed into a romantic outdoor room with a criss-cross canopy and candles for night-time illumination. The plant stand adds decorative detail.

left:

*This ingenious barbecue has been built into a disused chimney. A strawberry tree (*Arbutus unedo*), honeysuckle,* Pyracantha *and lacecap hydrangeas provide the backdrop for this rooftop dining room with its dramatic view of the surrounding skyline.*

West

coast style

THIS TYPE OF GARDEN captures the spirit of Californian open-air living where the garden is a true extension of the house. These gardens often reflect interior styling so that the boundaries between the two environments are merged. For example, where wooden flooring or wall cladding is used indoors, the same style and colouring may be picked up by decking or cladding used to cover raised beds and planters. The architectural backdrop doesn't have to be modern, but the lines should be clean and simple with an overall impression of spaciousness. In a very small garden this can be difficult to achieve. However, if you keep the walls and boundaries plain and cluster plant pots together to leave an open area of flooring, you can create a similar feel. Even better, avoid the clutter of small

pots altogether and just use matching troughs and one or two large specimen planters.

One way of strengthening the West Coast mood is with colour. Rich,

vibrant shades look perfectly at home in warm, sunny climates because of the quality

of light, but are harder to use successfully where the sky

is frequently overcast. In this case, limit your use of

bold eye-catching paintwork to just one section of wall,

e.g. an alcove, decking, a pergola or built-in troughs and

seating. Also, don't forget the possibility of introducing colour through fabrics used for

canvas awnings and cushion covers.

Wood is frequently used in the garden's construction and is often left

unpainted so that the natural colour and grain patterns can be appreciated. But you

are also just as likely to find it mixed in with ultra-modern materials such as chrome

and plastic resins.

Considerations of personal comfort are paramount, along with the ability

to entertain friends and family with ease. Ideally there should be ample built-in and

right:

Deep cornflower blue paintwork turns a triangular gable end into a stunning backdrop for this roof terrace. The design is modern yet relaxed with a mix of shrubs, perennials and annuals grown in terracotta pots of differing shapes and sizes. The seating area is sheltered from wind by tough plants – a rowan tree (Sorbus), Arbutus unedo, laurel (Prunus laurocerasus) and Pyracantha, an arrangement which also gives the more sensitive plants conditions in which they can prosper.

separate seating – benches, chairs and tables – but remember the design and colour of

furniture also has a significant influence on the look of the garden. Choose a well-

defined theme and keep to it. In favourable climates, not only is dining alfresco a

popular pastime, but so too is cooking. If you have room, turn part of your balcony

or roof garden into a mini kitchen area with a built-in barbecue and an awning or

canopy with adequate lighting so that you can use the facilities after nightfall.

Garden decoration tends to be confined to simple yet striking set pieces –

a modern sculpture or perhaps a mural. Natural sculpture is very much in keeping,

such as beautifully weathered driftwood or a grouping of large, smooth cobbles. Clever

use of spot lighting can turn quite a simple item into a dramatic focus for the garden

at night (see pg.125).

(see pg.125)

Add colour and decorative detail with plant containers, but whatever

material you choose, pick designs with a simple, bold outline and colour co-ordinate

the planting. Flowers are less important here than foliage, particularly plants with a

tropical flavour. If you are able to overwinter them, try some other tender subjects like

citrus trees and edible figs (*Ficus carica*) grown as standards. In cold, windy gardens it

is vital to establish some form of windbreak so that vulnerable plants have adequate

protection. Reasonably tough plants with

sculptural foliage and flowers include

hydrangeas, *Phormium tenax*, *Choisya ternata*,

laurel, *Arbutus unedo* (strawberry tree), *Rhus*

typhina (sumach), Euphorbia and day lily.

left:

A smart city roof terrace with wooden decking and matching planters containing Mediterranean and drought-tolerant plants in yellow, purple, silver and white. The overall effect is one of spaciousness and elegance.

right:

Relaxation is the overriding theme in this sheltered and secluded garden. Wooden decking is warm and comfortable for bare feet and makes the perfect surround for this jacuzzi.

Classical

grandeur

above:

Foliage breaks up the outline of the buildings behind and acts as a foil for these magnificent Parisian urns whose gold colouring adds a note of luxury. The red-leaved Cordyline *make suitably dramatic plant subjects.*

ONE DRAMATIC SET PIECE may be all that's needed to give your garden the required air of distinction – a neo-Classical wall fountain perhaps, a Greek urn on a plinth or an elegant statue. If you look in mail order catalogues you will find no end of designs and excellent reproduction pieces.

Fortunately many of these are made from lightweight fibreglass-reinforced resin which can now be made to appear like anything from stone to lead or weathered copper, and unlike solid stone or cast cement, you don't need to be too concerned about weight.

Site your chosen piece carefully. Brickwork can mar the effect and statuary often looks

right:

A bare wall is transformed by this classical fountain and symmetrical planting arrangement. The large mop-headed hydrangea acts as a visual anchor at the centre of the collection of potted plants and columns of sweet peas stand either side like sentinels more impressive against a leafy backdrop. Trompe l'oeil trellis panels are particularly enhancing and a false perspective arch will not only highlight the chosen piece, but also give the impression of a way through the wall, especially when the central panel is mirrored.

Symmetry is another device which can be used to emphasise the importance of a piece. Use a pair of matching pots planted identically to bracket a feature, for instance white Paris daisy standards in garlanded terracotta pots. A series of Versailles planters fitted with a trellis obelisk would also make a dramatic statement

against a plain wall, as would pots containing topiary figures. Use geometric shapes – spirals, cones and pyramids, spheres and ball-headed standards - to give the garden the appropriate architectural feel. You could even create an avenue of standards or clipped box globes in pots to form a visual connection between a viewing point and the feature in question. Specially designed frames covered with climbers can be used to create 'instant' topiary and some, like the Victorian wirework reproductions, can be considered works of art in their own right.

Clipped hedges can strengthen the design of a garden and emphasise its formality. Plant suitable subjects, e.g lavender, rosemary, cotton lavender, yew and pyracantha, in matching troughs or in long planters. Ensure that plants have an adequate water supply or their good looks may deteriorate. Dwarf box (*Buxus sempervirens* 'Suffruticosa') is ideal for creating clipped mini-hedges which can be used to mark out specific areas of the garden or to create a formal parterre effect.

Cottage *garden*

O F A L L G A R D E N S T Y L E S , this is probably the easiest to construct in the mind's eye – the thatched cottage surrounded by a picket fence, spires of hollyhocks and delphiniums, roses and honeysuckle around the door. Fortunately you don't need any of these elements to make a convincing cottage garden. It's not so much which plants you use as how you put them together. In cottage gardens of old, space was at a premium so fruit, vegetables and herbs for cooking and medicinal purposes were grown with flowers like snowdrops, primroses and violets. It is this jumble of plants which characterizes the cottage garden.

Wooden steps act like a tiered plant stand for a jumble of clay pots planted with a wide assortment of foliage and flower. This is a classic example of cottage garden style.

As a starting point, think about the backdrop. Modern brickwork can easily be disguised using square trellis panels stained or painted a soft blue perhaps. Wattle hurdles would also be very much in keeping as a screening material. Floors can be surfaced with anything which gives a country feel – random stone flags, brick laid in patterns, quarry tiles or wooden decking. Random groups of paving units in a gravel surround work well.

Use climbers of medium vigour including roses, clematis, honeysuckle and ivy as well as perennial sweet pea (*Lathyrus latifolius*) to

The slate roof, blue-grey paintwork and wooden decking provide a neutral backdrop for this vibrant array of flowering plants which includes cottage favourites like sweet peas, nasturtiums, snapdragons and geraniums.

left:

Trellis panels covered in ivy and climbing hydrangea provide a cottage-style backdrop for this roof garden, filtering out the view of the railings and brick wall behind.

right:

Plant stands can be used to display lots of small pots effectively and are useful space savers. This mix of herbs, edible flowers, medicinal plants and ornamentals is typical of cottage-style planting.

cover walls, railings and screens and surround windows and doors. To cover pergolas and archways, pick vigorous species together with grape vine and golden hop *(Humulus lupulus* 'Aureus') For shelter, combine trellis or wind break netting with a foreground of traditional cottage shrubs such as holly, pyracantha, cotoneaster and *Viburnum tinus*.

Make troughs from wood, either stained, painted or left to weather naturally. Unconventional containers such as paint cans in primary colours, storage jars in glazed stoneware, metal pails, or old tin baths also have rustic appeal.

Mix annuals, flowering perennials, herbs, salad vegetables and bulbs together and concentrate on scented and aromatic varieties. Choose dwarf or compact forms wherever possible to reduce the risk of wind damage. Although the emphasis is on flowers, try to avoid a summer bonanza which leaves the garden devoid of interest the rest of the year. Add winter berrying shrubs such as low-growing cotoneasters and for flowers, try *Jasminum nudiflorum*, scented *Daphne mezereum*, *Viburnum farreri* and hellebores. Bulbs such as *Scilla mischtschenkoana*, *Iris reticulata*, *Crocus chrysanthus* and *Narcissus* 'Tête à Tête' make an excellent show in late winter.

*This clever arrangement of
natural wooden decking
incorporates a shallow pool filled
with cobbles. Foliage plants
including* Griselinia littoralis,
*golden mock orange (*Philadelphus
coronarius *'Aureus'),* Fatsia
japonica, *Hosta and Iris provide a
wealth of contrasting shapes and
textures.*

Eastern *tranquillity*

above:

Use your oriental roof garden to display bonsai such as this gnarled old pine tree.

IN MANY WAYS oriental garden designs are ideal for balcony and roof spaces. You can easily create a scheme which is attractive but needs very little maintenance – perfect for busy city dwellers. The high proportion of evergreens and the harmonious design mean that these kinds of gardens are pleasing to look at year round, and wonderfully relaxing places to retire to after a hectic working day.

Certain materials are strongly associated with oriental gardens – natural wood and gravel for flooring, bamboo for screens, furniture and plant supports and ceramics for plant containers. Different areas of use in the garden can be highlighted

using contrasting materials. For example, you might want to mark out a place to sit with wooden decking and stand pots of plants on a surround of gravel. Or you could plan a gently curving stepping-stone pathway through gravel, which leads to a simple bench seat sheltered by foliage plants in glazed Chinese ginger jars.

Before you start, you will need to disguise features which reflect other styles or architectural periods: split cane fencing is ideal for this purpose. Use thick bamboo poles lashed together to construct simple trellising and windbreak panels or to create a decorative backdrop for plain, rendered walls. You can buy the raw materials from companies specialising in Japanese gardens.

Ornaments should be used sparingly and placed with care - perhaps a contemplative Buddha beneath the arching fronds of a large fern or a stone lantern lighting the way next to a path. Use strong colours for dramatic effect – traditional lacquer-red will stand out vividly against a largely neutral backdrop. Use it to highlight an architectural element such as a pergola or make a feature of a plant container by planting it with flame-red flowers.

The focus of this Japanese-style roof garden is the seating area with its chairs like wooden sculptures and low stone table. Split bamboo cane fencing provides a suitably oriental backdrop for the garden and highlights the plantings of bamboo, Fatsia japonica, *iris and ornamental sedge (*carex). *Other oriental-looking plants for containers include bergenia,* Pinus mugo, *camellia, magnolia and lacecap hydrangea*

Garden

theatre

ARDEN DESIGN has much in common with the theatre. Both are concerned with escapism, creating a world of make-believe, dazzling the viewer with spectacle and deceiving with artful trickery. Attention to detail is vital if the illusion is to succeed. This involves using the appropriate props and ensuring that any feature which doesn't fit in is removed or obscured.

In a garden you can let your imagination run wild and act out any fantasy. You can create gardens from a particular point in history, from favourite places visited on your travels, from films, books and even fairy-tales.

*The sun floor mosaic and 'throne'
with intriguing metal spheres set
into the arm rests bring a
mystical, other-worldly feel to this
garden and the twin box
standards give the throne even
greater significance. Clematis,
Viburnum opulus, roses,
Artemisia, herbaceous geraniums
and Cotinus provide a lush
backdrop and help screen out
any distractions.*

Follies were popular in Victorian times and although you almost certainly won't have room to build anything on a similar scale, you can construct stage sets which are just as evocative. All you really need is the right backdrop and some props to help set the scene. For example, if you wanted to immerse yourself in a Gothic fantasy and create the ruined courtyard of a medieval castle, you could commission treillage in the form of a series of pointed archways to run along the top of a parapet and give the impression of cloisters. Paint the walls to look like old faded and cracked plaster or crumbling stonework and attach a couple of heavy black wrought iron candle sconces. Age the scene further by applying a tracery of ivy using a stencil to give the impression that nature has begun to take over. Pieces of carved masonry, purchased from architectural salvage companies would add to the ruined look and reproductions of carved stone containers or a wall fountain would also be in keeping. Gothic-style furniture in wood or wrought iron is available for garden use, and for dramatic colouring and a touch of luxury, you could cover soft furnishings with fabric in deep

left:

The ram's head wall fountain and box topiary evoke an image of an Italian courtyard garden. You may only need one or two props like these to create a believable theme.

Another view of the plant hunter's garden complete with brass telescope, old radio and suitcase full of treasures. You probably wouldn't want to use anything of value outdoors, but it's well worth hunting in junk shops for the props to create your particular make-believe garden. Notice the 'ship's' railings with canvas panels lashed on to heavy gauge wires. This would be a relatively cheap and easy way to provide privacy and shelter.

midnight blue or regal red, patterned with gold stars, crowns or fleur-de-lys.

The wall described above is an example of trompe l'oeil, a French term which roughly translated means 'something which deceives the eye'. For more ambitious projects such as creating imaginary views, statuary or architecture, you may need to employ the skills of a set painter or specialist in murals.

However, there are easier examples of trompe l'oeil. You could, for example, create an air of mystery by suggesting a way through to another part of the garden. All you need to do it attach an old door in its frame onto a solid wall to give the impression of the continuing garden. Strengthen the illusion by placing a pair of planters on either side or by constructing an archway over the top and covering it with climbers. Mirrors can also be used to give the effect of a doorway or window but you need to be sure that there will be a suitable reflection of another part of the garden, otherwise the results can be very disconcerting. When using mirrors, it is particularly important to disguise the edges. Camouflage with foliage or set it within a false perspective arch or tunnel.

left:
This grand 'entrance' through to an adjacent garden is a fine example of trompe l'oeil. The rendered wall has been painted to look like a classical portico and the arched doorway is in fact a mirror which reflects the semi-circular pool at its base.

right:
The head of an ancient goddess keeps a watchful eye from an ivy-clad wall.

Hacienda
style

TO CREATE A GARDEN with a Latin-American or Spanish feel, you'll need a design which conjures up an image of heat and dust and unrelieved sun. Walls and built-in planting beds should be kept very simple. Disguise brickwork and breeze-blocks behind rough-textured white-washed rendering or rich terracotta coloured stucco. If you have a bare expanse of wall, introduce a Moorish theme by making a series of mock archways to give the impression of a cloistered courtyard – use wooden cut-outs, arched mirrors or simply paint them on. Wooden constructions such as pergolas and benches look the part when made

The views from this Spanish-style
roof garden are undoubtedly
magnificent, but would anyone be
foolish enough to choose the cat's
favoured look-out point?

from bulky, rough-sawn timber, stained dark brown. Doors should also have the same heavy feel with solid panels and chunky metal fittings.

Cover floors with pale stone flags or terracotta floor tiles. For a Moorish feel, use a solid block of decorative floor tiles with an Arabic design either to demarcate the main seating area or as a border. Panels of coloured tiles or ceramic mosaic can also be used to decorate alcoves and recesses, to line pools or cover work surfaces around a barbecue.

Ornate black iron-work chairs, tables and wall lamps or dark, carved wooden furniture strengthen the Hispanic mood. Soften floors, walls and seating with Mexican-Indian textiles woven in bold patterns and colours or use fabric with a Moorish motif.

In frost-free climates plant large specimen cacti. Certain varieties of *Yucca*, *Cordyline*, *Phormium*, *Sedum* and *Kniphofia* give a similar feel to the garden but will withstand cooler conditions.

above:
Black ironwork railings and ornate furniture make a strong contrast with the colourwashed walls and pale brick paving.

right:
Scarlet geraniums in simple clay pots stand out vividly against the dark woodwork and whitewashed walls of this hacienda-style building.

Colonial

influences

THERE IS A STYLE OF BUILDING which is characteristic of the

time when tropical locations like the West Indies, Africa, Australia and

the Far East were under colonial rule. It is usually of wooden

construction with shuttered windows and louvred doors which help to keep the building

cool, with wide balconies and verandas to sit out on at the end of the day. These

buildings were often beautifully decorated with intricately carved wooden barge boards

or wrought iron balcony railings. If you're lucky enough to live in one of these original

buildings, then you will probably want to create a garden in keeping with its history

below:

The lush, tropical-looking foliage on this New Orleans balcony stands out against a Caribbean colour scheme – watermelon-pink walls, saffron-coloured fabric and blue-grey louvred shutters.

and location. Of course if you want to re-create the feel of such a garden in a temperate climate, the hardest part will be finding plants with suitably sub-tropical looks which will survive the cold.

Part of the way round this would be to grow your houseplants indoors in the winter and to move them out on to the balcony or roof garden for the summer

left:

A garden in West Sussex, England designed to look like that of a plantation owner in the Far East! The bamboo in its ornately decorated pot acts as a geographical indicator and striking foliage plants including Sparmania africana, Aeonium *and blue-leaved* Echeveria *enhance the tropical mood.*

months. In pots and planters try the dramatic African hemp (*Sparmania africana*), *Aspidistra, Dracaena, Hibiscus rosa-sinensis,* succulents, bromeliads, figs including the rubber plant (*Ficus elastica*), foliage begonias and yuccas. In hanging baskets and wall pots, plant asparagus ferns, *Chlorophytum* (spider plant), Boston fern (*Nephrolepis*), *Scindapsus* and trailing *Tradescantia*.

Hardy plants which add a flavour of the tropical Far East include foliage varieties such as evergreen ferns, bergenias, *Iris foetidissima, Carex pendula* and especially bamboos. These plants, together with plain-leaved evergreen shrubs, make an excellent framework for the garden during the winter which can be added to in summer.

Evergreens with glossy, tropical-looking foliage are perfect for colonial style gardens. Common laurel (*Prunus laurocerasus*) is quite a tough plant and comes in useful as a first line of defence on a windy balcony. The false castor oil plant is particularly striking though it needs a more sheltered position, and the cabbage palm (*Cordyline australis*) and hardy Chusan or fan palm (*Trachycarpus fortunei*) also have a strongly tropical feel.

In the early summer look in garden centres for tall, large-leaved plants which are normally used as dot plants in bedding displays. These include Indian shot (*Canna*) which looks a little like a banana, abutilons, varieties of the castor oil plant (*Ricinus communis* – poisonous), love lies bleeding (*Amaranthus caudatus*), silk oak (*Grevillea robusta*) and *Eucalyptus globulus*.

Use wooden decking, shuttered windows and doors, hammocks, slatted bamboo blinds and draped mosquito nets to conjure up an image of the tropics. Decorate using objects indicative of your chosen country – for Africa you could display traditional wood carvings and water carriers made from gourds, for the Far East, ceremonial masks and planters decorated with Chinese dragons.

above:
Ornate cast iron balcony railings are a typical feature of the Victorian houses in the Paddington area of Sydney. Where space is restricted, hammocks offer a practical solution to the problem of seating.

right:
The plants in pots below the balcony are all common houseplants in cooler climates and could be used during the summer months to give a sheltered balcony or roof garden a jungle feel.

Cook's
potager

THERE IS NOTHING QUITE LIKE growing your own fresh vegetables, fruits and herbs and with planning, even tiny balcony gardens can produce a mouth-watering selection. Raised beds, large troughs and wooden half-barrels make excellent containers for growing fruit and veg because of the relatively large soil volume, but you can also use wall pots and hanging baskets for herbs and even ultra-compact cascading tomato varieties.

Sow small quantities of quick-maturing vegetables in patches at regular intervals to give a succession of produce. Certain vegetable varieties are ideal for this

technique. Try the many varieties of lettuce, as well as mustard, rocket, radish, kohl rabi, turnip and spring onions. Instead of growing vegetables to maturity, you can also use your growing space more efficiently by sowing closer together and harvesting early. Try beetroot, carrots and mini-cauliflowers, especially varieties described as 'early' or suitable for forcing. Vegetables including lettuce and spinach can also be grown as cut-and-come-again vegetables where successive harvesting of the young leaf is made.

Other compact vegetables which can be grown in containers include asparagus pea, mangetout and sugar peas, dwarf French beans (these can have attractively coloured pods) and dwarf cherry tomatoes. Utilize vertical space by growing runner beans or squashes, both of which can be highly ornamental. Several kinds of dwarf and compact-growing fruit trees and bushes can be grown in containers, together with climbers such as grape vines and hybrid berries. Strawberries are also easily grown in pots and can make an attractive edging for troughs and raised beds.

left:

Tubular steel hand rails and square grid mesh give a hi-tech feel to this roof terrace. Architectural plants like the Canary Island date palm and spiky yucca look well against a futuristic backdrop.

Modern
vision

right:

Victorian cast iron furniture, basket-weave terracotta pots and formal topiary are all elements associated with gardens of the past, but here the innovative use of colour gives this garden a distinctly modern feel.

IT IS NOT ALWAYS NECESSARY to use futuristic materials and designs to make a garden feel modern. It can simply be a case of using traditional or everyday elements in an unexpected way. Take, for example, a roof space in a period building with brick walls and typical architectural detailing. You could paint the whole of the façade surrounding the garden in just one colour, including bricks, masonry, railings, windows and doors, effectively simplifying the backdrop. Taking the example to the extreme, you could make the whole garden monochrome, by colour co-ordinating containers, furniture and the planting too.

Gardens with modern looks tend to give an impression of spaciousness and lack of clutter; they have a strong underlying design which is often highly geometric with straight lines and sharp angles. Planting follows a similar trend using shrubs and perennials with bold overall structure or sculptural characteristics. Clipped plant specimens and various geometrical topiary shapes also fit in very well with modern planting schemes despite having a strong association with period gardens.

below:

The stark white walls of this modern courtyard garden are softened by honeysuckle, ivy and other creepers and the greenery helps to create a cool and tranquil outlook.

Evergreens are important in the modern garden because they continue to provide structure even in winter when other gardens can look weak and untidy. Texture is far more important than colour and, as a result, foliage plants tend to take precedence over flowering varieties. Plants with an unusual texture, form or colour can be very striking in a modern setting, for example for a blue foliage theme you could try blue-leaved grasses like *Festuca glauca, Eucalyptus gunnei, Ruta graveolens* 'Jackman's Blue' (irritant), blue-leaved hostas and *Melianthus major.*

The way that plants and containers are arranged is another significant factor. For example, identical planters set at regular intervals along a boundary wall create a pattern which is extremely eye-catching and has much greater impact than a group of containers placed randomly.

Although you don't need to use hi-tech materials in the garden's construction, there are certain items which look modern mainly because you don't expect to see them outside or in a garden setting. Try visualizing the effect of tubular metal hand rails and square mesh grid infills instead of wooden trellis or fancy

wrought iron railings. As an alternative to terracotta and stone, think about using containers made from high-gloss resin or shiny metal. You may not have much luck tracking down unusual containers in the garden centre, so instead look in shops specializing in office furniture, DIY, kitchen equipment or interior design.

Lighting is another style indicator. Some modern light fittings have a sculptural quality, while others are very low key and may be almost invisible in daylight. If you have trouble finding the designs you want, it might be worth going to a mail order specialist or a reputable garden design firm.

The focal point of this avant-garde roof terrace is the willow-backed seat, its individual canes threaded with coloured beads. Empty mussel shells have a metallic appearance and make an interesting foil for the tall galvanized containers.

Provençal

charm

THE MERE WORD PROVENCE evokes a wealth of images – vineyards, sunflowers, crumbling stone farmhouses, olive groves, and fields of aromatic herbs and wild flowers shimmering in the heat haze. The question is, how to capture the essence of this magical region of France.

If the garden is sunny and reasonably sheltered, the best way might be via the choice of plants, but first you must decide what to plant in. Rectangular wooden troughs are quite easy to make. Use rough re-claimed timber and allow it to weather naturally on the outside, but use a preservative treatment on the inside and base to

right:

Scented geraniums, dainty white
marguerites and a pink rose
planted in a stone vase combine
to make a suitably rustic picture.
Farmhouse-style features like the
blue shutters and pale stone-effect
flags could easily be copied.

prevent rotting. Alternatively, for subtle colouring use a slate blue wood stain. Wooden half-barrels, reminiscent of wine making, would also be in keeping. The pottery of this region is typically chunky, functional and lacking in ornament save perhaps a roughly applied glaze. Search out containers with a similar look for both planting and decoration or choose plain terracotta pots and troughs.

left:
Sun-bleached wood and dry-stone walling are elements which complement each other admirably. Wild flower look-alikes such as this cultivated form of Viola tricolor *add to the countryside feel.*

Choose plants with aromatic foliage, especially the drought resistant silver- and grey-leaved shrubby herbs like lavender, *Santolina* (cotton lavender), curry plant (*Helichrysum italicum*), and *Artemisia* (wormwood). Other suitable silver-grey shrubs include *Phlomis*, *Senecio* 'Sunshine', *Ballota* and *Convolvulus cneorum*. The herbs oregano, thyme, sage, hyssop and chamomile also thrive in pots and you could plant troughs with a hedge of lavender or rosemary.

Annuals and tender perennials which have the look of wildflowers would also be in keeping, e.g. Californian poppy (*Eschscholzia*), dwarf cornflowers and marguerites, and for fun, why not grow a few dwarf sunflowers.

right:
Potted geraniums can always be relied upon to produce a brilliant display regardless of how hot and dry the conditions become.

Island

simplicity

above:

*Mediterranean blue paintwork,
white-washed walls and pots
of red geraniums immediately
bring to mind images of the
Greek islands.*

WHEN HOLIDAYING in the Greek islands and other coastal

Mediterranean destinations you cannot help but notice the

ingenious ways in which people garden with very limited

resources and space. Even old olive oil and paint cans are pressed into service, their

former life hidden by a fresh coat of paint. If you have a jumble of mismatched pots,

painting them in this way could turn them into a harmonious collection. This is not

the look to adopt if you like neat and tidy gardens. You'll see small clay or plastic

pots attached higgledy-piggledy to railings and walls, and plants apparently combined

An extraordinary collection of
fruit and vegetables, some real,
some fake decorates this corner of
a balcony garden. Rosemary and
other herbs grow in troughs and
pots below.

according to whim. There is rarely any attempt at colour co-ordination and flowers with bright, clashing colours jostle for attention.

The geranium is king in the Mediterranean, its brilliant blooms standing out vividly against the whitewashed rendering and blue or mint green woodwork. Other common pot plants include cacti such as Opuntia, the orchid cactus (*Epyphyllum*) and a variety of succulents. Many striking foliage plants are also grown, for example *Dieffenbachia* (dumb cane – poisonous), philodendron, Boston fern (*Nephrolepis*) and *Caladium* as well as flowering shrubs such as the ubiquitous oleander (*Nerium oleander* – poisonous). In colder climates all of these plants would normally be restricted to the house or conservatory.

A limited number of annuals can also be grown, such as the ice plant or Livingstone daisy (*Dorotheanthus*), marigolds and zinnias, but there is no reason why you couldn't grow many other kinds of sun-loving annuals to give a similar look and feel. The Marvel of Peru or Four o'clock flower (*Mirabilis jalapa*) is not widely available but is easy to raise from seed and the tubers can be overwintered in a frost-free place. This plant comes in a range of shades and gets its name from the

left:
During summer, some shelter from the heat of the day is necessary and this vine-covered pergola does the job perfectly.

right
This simply decorated balcony garden doubles as an alfresco dining room. Hurricane-lamps provide romantic lighting for night-time entertaining.

fact that the sweetly scented blooms open in the early evening.

Of course no Mediterranean garden would be complete without herbs and

sweet basil is a must for cooking, its amazing aroma released at the slightest touch. In

this type of garden, anything goes and you're quite likely to find tomatoes, aubergines

and courgettes growing amongst the flowers. Fruit trees including oranges, lemons, figs and apricots are often used to shade the small courtyard gardens, their stems usually painted white to match the walls. With the exception of citrus trees which must be kept frost-free in winter, most fruit trees and bushes can be successfully grown outdoors in large tubs year round.

Simple wooden pergolas covered in climbers provide relief from the heat of the day and cast dappled shade below. As well as grapes, a wide variety of flowering vines are grown including *Bougainvillea*, scented jasmine, Chinese trumpet vine (*Campsis grandiflora*), honeysuckle (*Lonicera periclymenum*), blue-flowered morning glory and the common passion flower. Such plants are rarely formally trained and are instead allowed to ramble over walls and cascade down from balconies, forming flowering curtains.

In the Mediterranean people sit outside until late in the evening during the long summer months, and eating and drinking are more often than not alfresco activities. The furniture for these outdoor dining rooms is usually very simple and unsophisticated – a couple of

left:
The owners of this tiny balcony have managed to cram in an amazing amount of potted geraniums, demonstrating admirably just what can be achieved in a truly tiny space!

left:

*Morning glory, Virginia creeper
and rambler roses festoon this
balcony garden and help to shade
the seating area within.*

below:

*These old olive oil cans have been
painted and re-used as plant
containers.*

straight-backed wooden chairs and a little table covered with a cloth

perhaps. To strengthen the rustic theme, instead of electric wall lights,

think about using candle-lamps or old-fashioned hurricane-lamps. Flooring

made from random stone pieces with the mortar painted white would also

give an authentic look, but for a tiny space, use smaller units such as

brick paviours or quarry tiles.

left:

*A minaret made from fibreglass
provides an interesting focal
point for this London roof garden.
Diamond trellis and ornate cast
iron furniture add to the
period feel.*

Period
piece

IF YOU HAVE A BALCONY or roof terrace with a distinctive period backdrop, there are several ways to enhance the architectural features by developing the garden along appropriate lines. Initially you may have to undo some of the modernizations and 'improvements' made by previous occupants and this could entail removing layers of paintwork, rendering or a false façade, or more serious restoration work which is the province of specialists and craftspeople. Bright, modern colour schemes rarely suit old-style buildings and although you don't need to reproduce the exact colour that would have been used on wood and metalwork of the time, it's a good idea to do some research into the period in question to give you some direction.

Plants are what make a garden, but you do need to exercise care to ensure

that they are not allowed to get out of hand and obscure too much of the period

detailing. Fortunately there has been a recent backlash against the gaudy, artificial-

looking modern cultivars, in particular those produced by bedding plant

growers, and you can now buy a wide range of varieties in gentle

water-colours and soft 'antique' shades. If in doubt, a scheme of white

flowers with green and silver foliage always works well. Herbs and

species of herbaceous plants, shrubs and climbers also often have a more

old-fashioned appearance than modern cultivars. Many nurseries specialize

in old varieties. However, 'old' most certainly doesn't always mean 'best' in terms of

ease of cultivation and long-lasting, weatherproof blooms, which are the exact

requirements for plants grown in containers on balconies and roof gardens! And, if you

have a yearning for old roses, search out some of the more compact modern cultivars

which have been bred to have similarly shaped flowers and colouring but which are

better behaved in terms of habit, disease-resistance and flowering performance.

left:

Elegant white Clematis montana *is the perfect complement for this Regency-style balcony, but take care that plants as vigorous as this do not mask too much of the fine architectural detailing.*

right:

Despite the fact that this façade is dripping with hanging baskets, the plants only serve to enhance the building's tremendous style, in no way obscuring its features.

City *heights*

FROM A BALCONY OR ROOF GARDEN, the bird's-eye view across the metropolis can be simply breathtaking. Modern skyscrapers mingle with historic buildings and the scene is dotted with patches of greenery. Raised up high, the sounds of the city are muffled and it's possible to feel detached from the hectic activity at street level. At night the cityscape is magically transformed and if you are at work all day, evenings will be the prime time for enjoying the garden.

City gardens often reflect the architecture around them which is likely to be a mix of modern and traditional. Through strong colour scheming and a well-

left:

A smart city balcony with views of the New York skyline. Notice what an impact the bold abstract design fabric has on the style of the garden and how well it complements the black wrought iron railings.

below:

Few gardens could boast a view of Sydney harbour bridge and the opera house! The designers of this balcony have made clever use of a mirror which reflects views of the park.

planned co-ordinated approach to design, construction and planting, such gardens can also have tremendous style.

For inspiration, begin by looking at the most striking features of some of your favourite city buildings. You can adapt certain elements of architectural detailing quite easily. For example, in many important municipal buildings, aspects of Greco-Roman styling are commonplace – columns, statuary, impressive porticos. There is a rhythm in the design of repeated patterns – perhaps a series of columns surmounted by identical carved figures and you could certainly mimic this look, albeit on a rather less grand

scale. Columns could be substituted by a series of tall, slim trellis panels attached to a wall and made to look more three-dimensional by fixing a large neo-classical head planter at the top of each. For night-time drama, use an uplighter at the base of the columns to throw the features of the face into sharp relief.

Another way of introducing a strong rhythm into the garden's design would be to fix a series of low trellis panels between taller posts along the top of a parapet. You can now buy a much greater range of trellis panel designs than the traditional square or diamond pattern and some have a distinctly modern feel. If the parapet is rather high, use panels with scooped tops so as not to obscure the view. Finish off the posts with wooden finials.

Simple modular constructions have a more modern feel, for instance rectangular planters separated by bench seats and planting can be an easy way to emphasise the symmetry of the design. At the centre of each you could use a clipped topiary standard or a sculptural foliage plant such as *Cordyline australis.* Surround with a softer, less well-defined planting of herbaceous perennials, annuals and trailers. Alternatively, instead of a central plant specimen, you could use a modern spiked light fitting such as a globe on a stem to similar architectural effect.

Colour can play a major part in creating the right mood for the garden. Certain paint colours, including black, deep Prussian blue, bottle green and dark cherry-red, are more strongly associated with city architecture and when used sparingly for highlighting certain features, can create a distinctly up-market feel. Furnishing fabrics can also be used to stylish effect.

This New York roof garden makes extensive use of wood in its construction and due to the design of the pergola and chair backs, has a somewhat oriental feel. If large enough, built-in planters can accommodate trees like these white-stemmed birch.

This magnificent solid wooden door makes a wonderful foil for the overhanging foliage from the balcony above. The fragrance from the roses and jasmine round the window must be heavenly, especially in the evening.

Faded

elegance

above:

A balcony in Rome looks out onto a piazza. The age-worn plaster wall makes a striking contrast with the flowers. Only the Swiss Balcony or Continental types of trailing geranium produce this effect.

Fine old buildings which have started to decay and crumble can make a wonderfully atmospheric and romantic backdrop for a garden. The distressed look continues to be a popular theme in interior design and there are numerous books on how to create the impression of age, mainly using a variety of specialist paint techniques and treatments.

But for this look to work, you do need some interesting architectural detail, representative of a period in history – without it, the façade can simply look shabby. Some pieces may have to be specially commissioned, for example carved wooden architraving for doors and windows, or decorative ironwork railings (consult membership listings of the various craft guilds). Alternatively, companies dealing in architectural salvage may have just what you're looking for.

Although smooth rendered surfaces are the most versatile when it comes to applying various paint finishes, brickwork can also be made to look old. One technique is to apply a patchy layer of cement rendering so that some of the brickwork is exposed here and there, leaving a weathered-looking surface. The difference between rendering and the under-surface can be further emphasised using different coloured paints. Old brickwork which has been painted several times in its life also has a characteristic look which can be mimicked. Apply a base coat and then use two or three slightly different colours to pick out small pieces of brick and occasionally a larger cluster of bricks. For best results, choose shades which blend easily so that no single colour stands out strongly from the rest.

A terrace in Sicily adorned with Bougainvillea *looks out over palms and pine trees.*
Because of the view and beautiful surroundings, there is little more that could be
achieved by additional planting or ornament.

Rendered surfaces can be painted with a darker background colour and then very lightly brushed over with a thinned down and paler version of the same colour so that most of the background shows through. This effectively emphasizes any surface imperfections. A similar effect can be achieved by mixing small amounts of a darker shade in with a lighter colour as you paint using random strokes. Apply a base coat first – preferably the same as the main colour. This is an ideal technique for achieving the gentle colourings of old weathered plasterwork.

Woodwork is also easy to age by applying different coloured coats and then sanding lightly to expose the colours beneath. Touches of gold paint brushed over decorative detailing suggests that the object was once covered in gold leaf. That same look of faded elegance and grandeur can be achieved using stencilling which has been sanded away in patches. Age new terracotta containers by colourwashing with white to mimic salts coming through to the surface. Sponge with green paint to suggest a covering of algae.

Practicalities

The themed chapters which precede this section provide numerous ideas on how to create a unique style or mood for your garden, but before you decide on any particular design, it's a good idea to ask yourself a few key questions.

What do you like and dislike about the existing balcony or roof space and its surroundings? How do you intend to use the garden – as a quiet and secluded hideaway in which to escape from the world outside, or as a place for entertaining friends, dining al fresco and enjoying the view? What is the prime consideration – plants or people? The answers to such questions will inevitably throw up a series of practical problems requiring solutions.

For example, if you desire seclusion on a balcony or want to blot out an ugly building, you'll have to think of a way to screen it, and if you intend to entertain outside at night, then you will need effective lighting. The following pages are mainly concerned with such practicalities.

First
steps

BEFORE YOU BEGIN ANY MAJOR CONSTRUCTION WORK, IT'S VITALLY IMPORTANT THAT YOU SEEK ADVICE ON WHETHER OR NOT PLANNING PERMISSION IS REQUIRED, EVEN IF ONLY RELATIVELY MINOR CHANGES ARE ENVISAGED. THIS IS NOT JUST FOR LEGAL OR AESTHETIC REASONS. SAFETY, OF COURSE, IS PARAMOUNT.

One flat roof or balcony may look very much like another, but could have widely differing structural specifications which only an expert would be aware of.

You or the contractor hired to do the construction work, must find out in the early planning stages how much extra weight your balcony or roof space can support. It may be possible to access the original architect's plans, but if in any doubt, the safest option is to discuss the design with a qualified structural engineer or architect. They will be able to advise on weight distribution, too. Normally, any major building work will be supervised by the architect or designer who originated the plans. If you are the designer and you are hiring contractors to do the work for you, it makes sense to have the plans looked over and possibly re-drawn by an architect before work commences, and also to use an architect for supervising the work. Make it clear from the outset which points concerning structural safety you wish to have addressed and word the contract accordingly.

Generally speaking, the floor space next to a wall can carry a greater proportion of the total load than can be supported at the centre. It may be possible to overcome the structural limitations of an existing roof by suspending a false floor from beams attached directly to the walls. When calculating the overall weight, bear in mind that soil and porous terracotta pots weigh considerably less dry than when filled with soil and saturated with water and, unless pruned to maintain size, plants increase in weight as they grow.

High stone balustrading makes a secure surround to this New York roof garden.

Another point which is well worth remembering is that all construction materials, furniture, plants, soil and containers will have to be brought up from ground level. It may perhaps be possible to winch certain items up the outside of the building, but if this is not an option, check first that there is sufficient space to manoeuvre materials around bends in the stair wells, in and out of lifts and through the apartment rooms.

SAFETY

It goes without saying that if you use the garden at night, there must be adequate lighting, particularly where there are steps, changes in level or skylights. A further prerequisite is to ensure that trellis, ornaments and plant containers are secured against wind and accidental knocks as anything falling from a balcony could easily injure someone on the street. Also, make sure that railings and other barriers are high enough for safety, solidly attached and if children are about, gaps are too small to slip through.

Railings fronted by planters enclose this roof terrace, making a safe and attractive boundary.

Environment

More tender plants may not survive as temperatures drop with the additional wind-chill factor. Another problem is that many plants lose moisture rapidly when exposed to strong winds and, when in containers, risk drying out altogether.

WIND AND TURBULENCE

The same conditions that make life difficult for plants can also affect our enjoyment of the garden. The answer is to provide some form of wind-break which is permeable to wind, but slows it down to an acceptable level. Solid screens create more turbulence so should be avoided where conditions are particularly severe. Wind-break netting with a 50 per cent permeability rating is a good first line of defence and black netting becomes virtually invisible when used as a backing for paler coloured wooden trellis. You can also mask netting with plants using tough, wind-resistant trees, shrubs and climbers around the margins to provide a more amenable microclimate for less hardy plants within.

Provided temperatures do not drop too far below freezing, plants listed as suitable for windy seaside gardens are ideal. Wind-resistant plants have a variety of ways to combat damage and these characteristics make them easy to spot, e.g. silver-grey plants with a dense covering of light-reflecting hairs or wool; plants with thick, leathery leaves with a waxy or glossy protective coating and ones where the leaf area is much reduced – either lots of small leathery leaves, e.g. *Escallonia* and low-growing cotoneaster or long, narrow or needle-like leaves such as

Here a clever combination of a large mirror and pale-coloured trellis creates a feeling of light and spaciousness on this shaded balcony.

pines, brooms (*Cytisus* and *Genista*) and blue- or grey-leaved grasses. Plants with flexible stems and pliable, strap-like leaves such as *Phormium* and *Cordyline* are also far less likely to be damaged. With flowering alpines, bulbs, herbaceous perennials and annuals, choose medium- and low-growing varieties with small, simple blooms and flexible flower stems.

HOT SPOTS

In some regions, relief from strong sunlight may be a more pressing problem than wind. Buildings reflect heat and light and towards the middle of the day, temperatures can become unbearable if no shade is present. Plants also dry out very quickly in these conditions and may become scorched or stunted in the dry atmosphere. Choose plants which are able to resist water loss, i.e. those with leaf characteristics similar to those described above. In addition, succulents and cacti thrive in hot sunshine though most won't survive sub-zero temperatures. Shrubs and herbs from Mediterranean countries are also suitable. For a mass of blooms in summer and drought-resistant qualities it is hard to beat geraniums (*Pelargonium*), but for variety try *arctotis* and *gazania*, *portulaca* and *mesembryanthemum* (*dorotheanthus*).

On a balcony or roof garden there's little chance of providing shade in the form of trees so man-made solutions must be sought. Collapsible canvas or sailcloth awnings are ideal as the fabric can be drawn across the seating area when needed. Another option is to build a pergola and cover it with vines and other sun-loving climbers to create dappled shade. Attach roll-down blinds at the sides for extra shade and privacy. In a sun-trap water can have a refreshing and cooling influence. A small, self-contained fountain or mini waterfall feature would suffice as just the sound of trickling water is extremely evocative and relaxing.

SHADE SOLUTIONS

Shade is less of a problem than wind or unrelieved sun. There are scores of plants which thrive in low light conditions, including many ferns, hostas and the false castor oil plant (*Fatsia japonica*), which in sheltered corners can be used to create a feeling of leafy luxuriance. In very exposed sites, stick to smaller leaved varieties. For height and to help create a barrier against wind, there are several tough, shade-tolerant evergreens to choose from. Many of the small-leaved varieties of ivy (*Hedera helix*) and several types of climbing honeysuckle (*Lonicera*) could be used to cover walls and trellis. Shrubs include holly (*Ilex aquifolium* and its cultivars), yew (*Taxus baccata*), laurel (*Prunus laurocerasus*) and the smaller leaved Portugal laurel (*P. lusitanica*), *Euonymus japonicus*, pyracantha and *Viburnum tinus*.

Brighten up shaded gardens by painting walls and by using trellis and railings in light colours (not necessarily white, as this can look rather harsh in shade). Choose pale coloured tiles or paving or paint timber decking a lighter shade. Follow the same guidelines with furniture, fabrics and plant containers – choose light colours and concentrate on plants with gold or variegated foliage and white, cream or yellow flowers. Mirrors sealed against the elements and set behind trellis panels on walls can also be very effective at reflecting light and space, as well as helping to make the garden seem much larger than it is.

Planning
the basic structure

TRY TO KEEP THINGS AS SIMPLE AS POSSIBLE AS THIS WILL HELP TO MAKE THE GARDEN FEEL LARGER AND STRENGTHEN THE OVERALL DESIGN.

When using trellis, keep to the same pattern throughout, i.e. all diamond or all square lattice; colour co-ordinate painted or stained surfaces such as pergolas, timber decking and built-in planters and try to keep to the same style, material or colour for pots, containers and ornaments.

LESS IS MORE

By using the same materials to construct or clad various structures in the garden, including flooring, you can create a fluidity of line which lets the eye travel across the scene without interruption or distraction. This creates a sense of space and works particularly well where the construction is modular, e.g. built-in seating flanked by raised beds around the edges of the garden or an island feature consisting of raised planters, seating and a shallow pool all set at different levels, but following the same basic design.

LINKING THEMES

When deciding on a particular colour scheme or design, it's helpful to consider your surroundings. You may want to reflect or complement the style of your building or any buildings which are in view from the garden. A scheme which is completely at odds with its surroundings may feel out of place and begin to jar after a while. If

Choosing similar colour schemes and construction materials for the garden helps to blur the boundaries between inside and out.

above: *A decking seat doubles as a child's sand pit. A similar arrangement could be used to create extra storage.*

right: *Long, narrow planters running along the base of trellis or railings take up relatively little floor space.*

it blends in, then the eye takes in not only the garden, but also the surrounding landscape creating an impression of a much larger space. Of course, if your aim is total seclusion, then this will not be such an important factor.

When dealing with very small gardens, a good trick to remember is one used by interior designers who link the decor of adjacent rooms to make the overall space appear larger. For example, if your living room looks out onto a balcony, you can visually extend the room outdoors by choosing similar colours, construction materials and fabrics, even plant containers, furniture and ornaments. Indoor and outdoor 'rooms' can also be linked physically by way of a simple pergola or canvas awning attached to the wall and stretched out across the garden. This acts like a ceiling, giving the impression of enclosure and further emphasizing the room-like quality of the garden.

SPACE SAVERS

With small-scale gardening, it is important to get the framework right from the start, i.e. the walls, floors, screens and dividers, raised beds, seating and so on. You can't afford to have 'dead space' – every square metre counts. On a tiny balcony, you may need some ingenious ideas for solving problems such as where to store gardening equipment, toys, cushions and so on, where to sit and eat or prepare food.

One of the best solutions for lack of storage is to make built-in seating with hinged, weatherproof lids and a hollow space beneath. A child's sand pit fitted with a lid can also double up as a place to perch or rest drinks. Fold-down tables fixed to the wall are ideal for food preparation next to a built-in barbecue. Tables and chairs can be of the collapsible, fold-flat variety, washing lines can be wound back into the wall for storage and a wide variety of plants in containers can be mounted on walls or railings, thereby freeing up valuable floor space. Small water

features can also be wall-mounted (see 'Ornaments' section).

PRIVACY AND ENCLOSURE

If you have good views from your balcony or roof garden, you're unlikely to want to sacrifice them for privacy. On the other hand, if you feel uncomfortable in the garden because of being overlooked, then you will need some kind of screening. A good compromise is to create a sheltered sitting area in one part which doesn't interfere with the best elements of the view – a church spire or other architectural landmark perhaps, a group of trees or a glimpse of water.

Gardens don't have to be completely enclosed, if they are, they can feel rather claustrophobic. You can leave gaps through which to view the world outside and you can even deliberately frame parts of the view using metal or wooden archways or trellis panels with 'windows' cut through the centre. If the garden is overlooked from above, consider covering the seating area with some kind of overhead awning or climber-covered pergola.

Keeping out prying eyes won't necessarily require a completely solid barricade. Sometimes all that's needed is to baffle the eye with a partial screen, e.g. trellis panels covered with climbers, or a grouping of shrubs,

bamboos and small trees grown in tubs and containers.

If you want a balcony or roof garden to feel more like an outdoor room, but don't want to surround it with solid 'walls', a pergola built over the whole or part of the garden will create a false 'ceiling'. It's also possible to create a sense of enclosure by erecting a framework of upright struts around the boundary, linked across the top by beams. These could be turned into archways by fitting shaped trellis pieces at the top between uprights set around 4 or 5 feet (1.2 or 1.5 metres) apart. Covered with trailing climbers, this boundary would create a soft and pretty effect for relatively little cost.

Finally, solid boundaries may be necessary to screen off an unpleasant outlook or to make the garden secluded and private. If this is the case, try to make the most of the decorative potential of any screening used – see 'Decoration Without Plants'.

POWER AND WATER

Once you know roughly where seating, planters and so on are to go, you'll need to map out the positioning of garden lighting and where best to run the cabling for this and any other power points, e.g. for operating running water features. All electrical fixtures and fittings must be outdoor specification, i.e. sealed against moisture ingress. Employ a qualified electrician for this work. If you plan to fit automatic irrigation, use a hose pipe or need a convenient point to fill a watering can, then you'll also have to think about plumbing. Associated with that is the question of drainage – where is the excess water from rainfall and plant containers going to drain to? It's inadvisable to allow it to collect in pools; it should drain away quickly and efficiently. You may not be very popular if you allow it to simply pour off the edge of the balcony or run down your neighbours' walls!

Container *gardening*

AS A GENERAL RULE, THE BIGGER THE POT OR PLANTER THE BETTER. SIZE OF POT, AND HENCE SOIL VOLUME, BECOMES CRITICAL ON WINDY AND EXPOSED BALCONIES AND ROOF GARDENS WHERE PLANTS TEND TO LOSE WATER VERY RAPIDLY.

Large planters are also useful in that they allow you to garden more conventionally, combining a variety of plants giving the effect of a mini-border. Trees, shrubs and climbers are better off as their roots tend to become restricted in smaller pots and this slows down the rate of shoot growth. Greater soil volume also helps to protect the roots of vulnerable plants from freezing.

It's not a good idea to plant a very small specimen on its own into a large container however – plants should be potted on as the rootball expands otherwise the excess soil around it can become stagnant, causing the roots to die off. The answer is to plunge several small pots up to the rim in larger pots filled with potting mix and to grow them together until they reach a suitable size for individual planting.

CHOICE OF CONTAINER

You can only use small or shallow pots successfully if you are able to water at least once a day, particularly during hot spells or if you plan to use succulents, e.g. *Sempervivum* (house leeks) or other drought-resistant varieties (see 'Hot Spots'). Plants in hanging baskets are particularly vulnerable to drying out, so unless using self-watering types, don't try anything smaller than 14 in (36 cm) in diameter. Wall-pots free up floor space, but on a hot, sunny wall can lose moisture rapidly. Rather than individual pots, it might be better to try troughs mounted on brackets or large manger-style baskets suspended from screws which have a much larger soil volume and are therefore less vulnerable to drying out.

LIGHTWEIGHT REPRODUCTIONS

With weight a primary consideration, it makes sense to choose lightweight containers wherever possible, especially where you plan to use very large pots and planters. The quality of plastic and fibreglass reproductions of stone, wood and terracotta varies considerably, but at the more expensive end of the market, the results can be very convincing, e.g. plastic copies of white- or green-painted wooden Versailles planters, where even the wood grain looks like the real thing. When planted up, it can be almost impossible to tell them apart.

Most plastics eventually become brittle with prolonged exposure to sunlight, so it's well worth looking for ones which state that they are resistant to ultra-violet degradation. The other drawback is that plastic versions of stone and terracotta don't weather and age attractively like the original pots they are modelled on. You can, however, use a mix of ordinary artists' acrylic paints to mimic the aged effect and also to make white plastic pots and urns look more like stone ones. Refer to books on paint effects and interior decoration for the various techniques.

Shiny metal flower buckets make eye-catching containers for a modern garden setting.

MODERN ALTERNATIVES

If you're looking for ultra-modern style, pots made from plastic or plastic reinforced with fibreglass come into their own. Once again, better quality productions can look very smart indeed, coming in an exciting range of colours and textures. Fibreglass is an exceptionally strong yet lightweight material, useful for large troughs and planters and if you can't find the shade you want, it can be painted to match your particular colour scheme. If your existing container collection consists of pots in a wide range of styles and finishes, consider painting the whole lot in the same shade to introduce a note of unity. You could also be really innovative and cover cast concrete, ceramic or terracotta pots with a mosaic of broken coloured tiles mixed with mirror tile shards. Metal containers made from zinc and aluminium are also becoming more popular for use in modern gardens. You won't find too many in the garden centres though – it's best to look in shops or departments specializing in interior design and decoration. Make sure there are sufficient drainage holes in the base before planting.

Wicker baskets provide another option for planting, but need to have a waterproof lining of some kind to keep the material as dry as possible and

prevent rotting. One of the best ways to use them is with plastic pot liners which can be lifted out and exchanged when the display is over. Wicker pot covers are ideal for gardens with a country feel.

ANTIQUE LOOK

For certain period-style gardens it's worth searching in antique shops and second-hand stores to find the right kinds of troughs and pot covers to create an authentic look, e.g. elegant wirework troughs for a romantic Edwardian-style garden or decorative plant stands made from cast iron for country or cottage-style plots. Fortunately there are companies who manufacture excellent reproductions. However, unlike copies of pots made from plastic, these are unlikely to be much cheaper! Reproductions of stone and terracotta pots and wall planters are readily available, but tend to look rather raw. You can produce an aged effect on cast concrete by painting in the contours with dark grey artist's acrylic paint and afterwards sponging the same shade over the whole surface. For terracotta, apply a wash of diluted white acrylic paint to give the effect of salts coming through to the surface.

SELF-WATERING

If you're not around to water pots on a regular basis, then self-watering containers, including hanging baskets, are one solution. The better kinds have a gauge which shows how much water is left in the reservoir. After planting and watering in, it just becomes a matter of keeping the level topped up via the watering tube. The plants draw moisture up through the soil from the base as and when they need it, which is useful if you have a tendency to overwater. Be sure to buy pots designed for outdoor use unless they are in a very sheltered position.

Plant *selection*

YOU CAN GROW VIRTUALLY ANY KIND OF PLANT IN A CONTAINER, INCLUDING TREES, PROVIDED THE POT IS BIG ENOUGH. SOME FARE BETTER THAN OTHERS HOWEVER. PLANTS WITH AN EXTREMELY VIGOROUS ROOT SYSTEM QUICKLY RUN OUT OF SPACE AND NEED FREQUENT DIVISION AND RE-PLANTING IF THEY ARE TO THRIVE.

Whereas most plants will stop growing when the roots have filled the container, some types, e.g. certain bamboos, continue to expand and eventually crack the walls through pressure build-up.

To avoid making expensive mistakes, it's essential that you find out what the likely temperature range is for your area – don't forget to calculate for wind-chill on exposed balconies and roof gardens. If you don't have overwintering facilities such as a greenhouse or conservatory, tender plants will have to be considered as a seasonal treat and discarded when the

display is over. Remember though, if you use tough plants as an outer defence, you can often grow more tender sorts in their shelter. Factors like sun and shade tolerance must also be taken into account if you want to ensure success (see 'Hot Spots' and 'Shade Solutions').

For best results, choose plants which have already been acclimatized to conditions outside. The shock of being moved from a warm, sheltered and humid environment to a cold, wind-blown balcony can prove fatal. Buy sensitive plants in late spring or early summer when conditions are more favourable, so that they have the

Evergreen shrubs like these sculptural fatsias *provide year round colour and interest. Introduce them into the garden in late spring so that they have sufficient time to acclimatize before winter.*

whole of the summer and autumn to toughen up and establish before winter. Try to select young, bushy and healthy plants and avoid any which show signs of neglect or which are badly root bound. When buying expensive, mature specimens and larger topiary pieces, seek advice from the nursery beforehand and think twice about making the purchase if they won't offer you some kind of guarantee.

SOIL

Certain plants require quite specific conditions and may die if these are not provided. For example, there are those which require acid soil, e.g. *pieris*, *rhododendron* and *camellia*, and these must be planted in lime-free or ericaceous compost and watered with lime-free water – rain water is ideal. Although peat and coir-based mixtures weigh less than soil-based compost, the latter is best for long-term plantings as organic elements degrade over time, causing the soil structure to collapse. This process occurs more rapidly in warm, moist conditions. Another problem is that peat and coir-based mixtures are difficult to re-wet once they have dried out. And one final point to remember is that in windy gardens, pots containing heavier soil-based compost are less likely to be blown over. Certainly if you are planting trees and large shrubs, use a soil-based mix recommended for mature plants, to avoid having to re-pot these unwieldy plants at some point in the future.

DRAINAGE

Succulents and cacti need a free-draining, gritty mix as do most alpines. You may need to add extra grit to loam-based composts to provide the right consistency. Whatever soil you use, leave room at the top to act as a water reservoir so that water doesn't just pour off before soaking in and make sure that there is a good layer of drainage material at the base to allow excess moisture to escape. This is especially important for large containers which dry out less rapidly – few plants enjoy having their roots in sodden compost. The term 'crocking' refers to the old practice of placing a piece of broken clay pot over the drainage hole to prevent soil clogging it up. If you do not have a supply of 'crocks' to hand, instead cover the hole with a piece of fine nylon mesh (e.g. wind-break netting), then cover with a 1-2 in (2.5-5 cm) layer of gravel before adding the soil.

Considerably lighter alternatives are polystyrene packaging chips or broken up plant trays. This material is also useful as filler for the lower portions of unusually tall, slim pots where plant roots rarely reach beyond the top two thirds. It's a good idea to raise pots on 'feet', otherwise on flat surfaces, the base can make a complete seal with the floor preventing drainage. If you use pot saucers or drip trays, don't allow plants to stand in water for any length of time, especially in winter – pour away the excess.

PLANT SUPPORT

Climbers often need some initial training to get them to latch onto the trellis or netting or attach themselves to walls. They are usually bought trained up a single cane. Free the individual stems, fan them out and re-attach to the netting. Use canes to bridge the gap if they don't quite reach. Continue to tie in the stems as they grow until they are self-supporting. With climbing roses, other scrambling plants and lax-stemmed shrubs, regular fastening in of the stems to trellis or wire supports is vital to avoid wind damage. When training plants up onto pergolas, first cover the posts with clematis netting so that the stems can grip on more easily and so that you have something to tie them to. Climbers don't have to be grown against walls and fences. Trained up cane wigwams, topiary frames or trellis obelisks, they can provide useful height contrast amongst low–growing plants.

Other plants including herbaceous perennials, bulbs and annuals may also need protection against the buffeting effects of the wind. Put in place proprietary wire supports when the plants are still small so that they grow through the mesh, or push in twiggy sticks. For single stems such as tall lilies, use individual wire supports or tie on to split canes.

WATERING AND FEEDING

If you have lots of pots and planters to look after, you may need something more practical than a watering can.

If you have a large number of containers to water, consider installing a nearby water supply or automatic irrigation.

Hose pipes can be fitted with spray guns which have on-off hand triggers to prevent waste. You can also get long lance attachments for reaching wall pots and hanging baskets with ease. Automatic irrigation systems are ideal if you are unable to water regularly and can be manually operated or attached to a timer switch for when you are away. You can also insert fertilizer tablets into the mechanism so that feeding is carried out simultaneously. These systems are rarely as accurate as good hand watering however. Even though you can adjust the individual drip nozzles to give more or less water, it's still worth checking now and then that the plants are getting what they need. One good trick with unglazed terracotta is to line the pot with plastic sheeting (e.g. a dustbin liner) to prevent moisture being lost through the walls. Do not cover the drainage holes.

During the summer months, large quantities of water pass through the soil in pots and this leaches out nutrients which must be replaced to prevent starvation. Liquid fertilizers tend to give the best results for flowering annuals, but if you don't have time or tend to forget to feed, you can also use slow-release fertilizers which are added at the beginning of the growing season. They are available as granules which can be sprinkled on the surface or mixed in with the soil, or as spikes or tablets which are pushed into the soil around the plants. Follow manufacturers' instructions and don't be tempted to use a higher dose in the hope of getting better results. You may scorch the roots or cause an abundance of tall, soft, sappy growth which is very vulnerable to wind damage and a magnet for insect pests!

MAINTENANCE

Plant displays in small gardens tend to need more grooming than in larger plots because everything comes under much closer scrutiny. Keep on top of dead-heading and removal of other debris and clear away seasonal plants as soon as they have finished flowering.

On windy, exposed balconies the main tasks will be keeping up with watering and staking and securing loose plant stems. You are unlikely to have many problems with flying insect pests, but expect to suffer some plant losses through wind and cold damage. Cut dead stems back to living tissue to promote re-growth. In hot dry conditions, mist foliage with water and dampen down paving to increase the

To keep displays looking as fresh as this, you will need to devote a certain amount of garden time to basic maintenance.

humidity around plants. Grouping pots together also helps to create a more moist microclimate and makes maintenance easier too. Air pollution in cities can deposit a sooty layer on evergreen foliage, turning glossy leaves dull. Every now and then it is a good idea to clean it off using a fairly strong jet of water and wipe over large leaves with a damp cloth.

Check for plants which need potting on or which have already become root bound. These tend to be noticeable by their need for very frequent watering and usually have roots poking out through the drainage holes. Use a pot which is only one or two sizes larger. When you want to keep a plant in the same container, you can replenish the soil at the start of each new growing season by carefully scraping loose soil from the roots and replacing it with fresh compost.

In the autumn, prepare delicate, non frost-free pots and tender plants for the coming winter. Wrap pots in hessian sacking stuffed with straw or use several layers of plastic bubble wrap to keep frost from penetrating the root ball. Evergreens are particularly vulnerable to damage if the root ball freezes when cold spells are combined with strong winds. This draws moisture out of the foliage which cannot be replaced by the roots and leads to damaging desiccation.

You can protect shoots by wrapping in layers of hessian, plastic bubble wrap or horticultural fleece. Fleece is also useful for protecting flower and vegetable seedlings and young plants during cold snaps at the start of the season.

SEASONAL INTEREST
Ring the changes by swapping around portable pots and planters now and then to create different groupings. It's also a good idea to move flowering plants into a more prominent position as they come into bloom. Although the majority of your planting may consist of evergreen plants which look very similar year round, you can introduce splashes of seasonal colour in the form of hardy annuals sown direct into pots and with bulbs. Brighten up the front of large troughs by plunging in potted bedding plants or bulbs. There's usually some room around the edges of shrubs and trees in containers to squeeze in a few dwarf bulbs such as *crocus* and *Scilla siberica*. Early flowering varieties are especially welcome around deciduous shrubs.

One way of ensuring that your favourite pots are always worth keeping on display is to fit them with removable liners – any cheap plastic

Bulbs create a welcome splash of colour in spring and most of the common varieties are easily grown in containers.

early dwarf daffodil Tête à Tête and then lily-flowered tulips and fluffy blue *Muscari comosum* 'Plumosum'.

DISPLAYING FOR EFFECT

Most gardens are decorated with a wide range of plants – trees, shrubs, herbaceous perennials, alpines, bulbs and annuals. The best looking borders are planted with contrasting varieties in large swathes or well-defined blocks. The same principle can be applied to floor displays made up entirely of plants in containers. Plant larger individual pots with a shrub or tree, or

pots will do. A whole series can be planted up with annuals, herbaceous plants and bulbs and kept in reserve, so that you have a succession of flowers in the same decorative cover throughout the year.

For long-lasting bulb displays in spring, plant in layers according to the required planting depths of the different kinds. You don't need to worry about planting bulbs on top of one another as they simply grow round any obstacles. A display could start off with a *Crocus chrysanthus* variety mixed with dwarf iris, followed by the

above: *Ring the changes by introducing pots of hardy annuals and tender bedding plants to permanent displays.*

right: *It's hard to believe that all the plants in this rooftop garden are grown in pots. Clustering pots together like this gives the effect of a thriving garden border.*

fill up the pot with a single variety of herbaceous perennial, bulb or bedding plant. Group smaller pots of the same variety together for greater impact. Position container-grown plants to create maximum contrast in form and texture, and don't forget to take into account the foliage of flowering

varieties which will almost certainly be on display for longer than the blooms.

Stagger different sized pots with taller ones at the back, shorter ones at the front. Consider the possibility of growing dwarf bulbs, ground-cover plants, succulents and alpines in shallow pans and troughs right in the foreground. However, don't be too rigid about height ranking, and bring some taller specimens forward to break up the line.

There are several ways to achieve height without taking up a lot of growing space. For instance, you can grow annual climbers such as sweet peas and runner beans up cane wigwams, and for strong vertical contrast, try bamboos and tall ornamental grasses, such as varieties of *Miscanthus sinensis* and *Stipa calamagrostis*.

The most dramatic results come from keeping planting to a well-defined colour scheme, and using a minimum number of varieties in adjacent pots. For a strongly formal look, space identical pots equidistantly in a straight line in front of a wall or on top of a parapet. You can also use a series of identical pots positioned at regular intervals to punctuate mixed pot plantings, which are otherwise

lacking in form. Evergreen plants with a bold outline such as a row of clipped box topiary globes would be ideal.

Enthusiastic gardeners often have particular plant favourites, e.g. herbs, alpines, bonsai or scented geraniums, which they collect as a hobby. Such a collection could become a real feature

Tiered plant stands are an excellent space-saving way to display smaller pots and favourite plant specimens.

of the garden, but careful thought should be given to the display. One way of doing this is to set the pots out on a staggered plant stand made of wood or metal. Wooden stands are easy to make and take up very little floor space so are ideal for balconies.

Decoration
without plants

BECAUSE OF THE RESTRICTIONS OF SPACE, THERE ARE ONLY SO MANY PLANTS WHICH CAN BE FITTED IN, SO IT'S A GOOD IDEA TO EXPLORE SOME OF THE MANY OTHER WAYS OF DRESSING UP THE GARDEN.

DECORATING WALLS

Adding a decorative façade to plain brick or rendered walls can make all the difference to the look of a garden. Simple trellis panels fixed at regular intervals and stained or painted in attractive shades make effective camouflage for dull walls. Exterior paints and stains now come in an exciting range of shades. Wood doesn't have to be brown – it can be stained or painted blue, for example, and walls can be painted in virtually any shade. Use colour to enhance the mood or design of your garden. For example, white and terracotta are associated with hot, sunny climates, while soft blues, greens and greys evoke memories of the ocean.

If you plan to train climbers up trellis panels, you'll get better results if you leave a gap between trellis and wall, fixing the panels to wooden battens. This is a wise move as it makes for easy training and access for maintenance. Decorative trellis or treillage is available in a wide range of shapes and designs, including simple trompe l'oeil pieces which create false perspective and make the garden feel bigger than it is. You can also buy large wooden cut-outs or silhouettes in a variety of designs. Bold topiary shapes like lollipop standard trees or cones in square Versailles planters are easily made from sheets of marine-quality plywood cut with a jig-saw and then stained or painted.

If you have some artistic talent, you could try your hand at a mural. For some of us this may be just too daunting a prospect, although copying a simple design onto the wall using a square grid as a guide, makes the process a lot easier. However, some paint techniques are relatively simple. Stencilling is one of them. Stencilling specialists make patterns which range from simple foliage and flowers to architectural elements such as columns and archways. One idea is to give the impression of a climber-clad wall when the actual plants are still quite small, or to fill in gaps where it would be difficult for plants to grow. You don't need to be terribly accurate. Just the impression of foliage in darker and lighter shades of green is enough to fool the eye, especially if painted behind trelliswork or on walls around existing plants.

Wall mosaics are also great fun to experiment with. Patterns using sea shells are popular and you could also try your hand at a Gaudi-style design using shards of colourful ceramic tiles. Attach with adhesive cement.

Metal, ceramic and wooden wall plaques and sculptures add texture to a wall and, depending on the subject, can be very dramatic. Wall-mounted water features such as animal heads or masks from mythology spouting water into a small reservoir can also be tremendously eye-catching. Other more theatrical effects include building a decorative arch or classically-inspired

portico over a very ordinary doorway or doing the same thing around a full length mirror, giving the illusion of a way through to another garden. Wood can easily be painted to look like carved stone, so this doesn't need to be an expensive exercise. Another idea is to fix colourful shutters around

Warm terracotta tiles with a contrasting geometric pattern make an eye-catching feature on this roof terrace.

windows. It doesn't matter if they don't actually work!

DECORATING FLOORS

The potential for exploiting the decorative qualities of flooring should not be overlooked. Timber decking, for example, opens up a number of interesting design possibilities. It is extremely versatile and can be used to create changes in level which can

enliven a flat expanse of roof, e.g. upper and lower decks linked by steps or staggered seating/sunbathing plinths. As decking is raised off the ground slightly with gaps between the planks, any excess water drains through relatively quickly. Another advantage of this construction is that it allows you to hide away cabling and pipework. The main disadvantage is cost. Decking pieces can be cut to create patterns and the design picked out using different shades of paint or wood stain. You can even use large simple stencils to transfer designs on to the wood giving an effect similar to tiled or mosaic floors.

In any floor covering exercise, there are always a few awkward gaps to contend with. Try turning this to your advantage by leaving a border around the edges of paving or decking and filling it with small cobbles (real or coloured ceramic imitations), gravel and even coloured glass beads or marbles. This is also a good way to camouflage ground-level irrigation pipes or electricity cables as it allows easy access if there is a problem.

Frostproof floor tiles are thin and relatively lightweight, and come in a wide range of patterns and styles. These can be quite expensive but are ideal for surfacing small floor areas where larger units would seem out of scale. They are easy to keep clean, but can become slippery when wet so take care where you use them. Another lightweight and easy-to-handle flooring product is the slatted wooden paviour. These quickly transform the look of black bitumen sealant or lacklustre concrete on a flat roof. More conventional looking slabs and paviours made from lightweight materials or as thinner-than-normal versions are also available. Again, these can be laid across the whole area or in abstract patterns set within a general covering of gravel. The contrast in texture can be very attractive indeed and will almost certainly work out cheaper. Other flooring focal points can be created using pebbles or coloured ceramic shards arranged in bold mosaic panels replacing ordinary paving.

SCREENS AND DIVIDERS

There's no reason why screens can't be decorative as well as functional and add something to the look of a garden. Modern city balconies are often surrounded by very ordinary looking iron bars which you'd have few qualms about covering over, whereas the ornate railings of some period buildings add greatly to the charm of the garden. In this case, it might be better to use plants in pots, troughs and hanging baskets to give the garden a little more privacy. Standard 6 x 6 ft (1.8 x 1.8 m) fencing panels are not really practical for screening off balconies and roof gardens, and besides there are more attractive options.

One way to create privacy between adjoining balconies for example is to erect a screen made from coloured canvas or sailcloth, lashed to a tubular metal frame. You can get all the necessary bits and pieces such as brass eyelets and nylon rope from a ship's chandlers. The same method could also be used along the boundary. Another light-coloured and very versatile screening material is Riviera fencing made from reeds or split bamboo canes. This is very lightweight and can be used purely for camouflage, attached to more functional fencing behind. It particularly suits gardens with an oriental or seaside flavour. Bamboo poles lashed together to make square or diamond trellis also work well as a garden room divider or as a decorative facade. Another form of lightweight fencing which can be made to measure is the wattle hurdle, woven

DIY trellis panels can be manufactured at far less cost using roofing lathes from a builders' merchant. Another type of do-it-yourself fencing which is quick and easy to construct once the framework is secure consists of thin wooden fencing planks nailed between parallel struts. Leave regular gaps so that air and light can still pass through and attach either horizontally, vertically or diagonally. You can even alternate upright or horizontal blocks along the length of the screen or set the planks in a diamond design.

Large planting troughs with trellis panels attached placed along the boundary, either inside the wall or on top of the parapet, instantly create privacy. And, when the plants and especially the climbers start to grow, the feeling of enclosure and seclusion becomes even stronger.

Finally, if you have a pergola, why not utilize the upright struts to attach trellis panels so that you can create a more intimate and sheltered place to sit and eat.

from willow stems. This makes a very natural-looking backdrop for plants and works well in a number of situations, blending in with other construction materials such as metal surprisingly easily.

Highly decorative treillage is available in designs to suit any requirement, whether it's an elegant arbour or set of arched panels to block out the view. Don't forget the finials for the tops of fence posts to create the whole period effect.

One useful point to bear in mind when using ready-made trellis panels is that it is far easier to paint or stain and preserve them before they are put into position. Lie the sections flat on the ground or prop against a wall with layers of newspaper to catch the drips.

Drill pilot holes and use screws to attach trellis panels to their wooden supports. If you hammer in nails, you risk splitting the thin struts and it makes it harder to dismantle the pieces for maintenance at a later date.

Outdoor *living*

IF CHOSEN MAINLY FOR AESTHETIC REASONS, FURNITURE CAN BECOME RATHER LIKE A PIECE OF SCULPTURE. A WELL-DESIGNED CHAIR OR BENCH SEAT PAINTED IN AN EYE-CATCHING SHADE AND SET IN A PROMINENT POSITION CAN HAVE TREMENDOUS VISUAL IMPACT.

Try to select pieces of furniture to suit the style and mood of your garden – simple wooden kitchen chairs or wicker perhaps for cottage-style gardens, tubular metal framed chairs or plastic for an ultra-modern setting, reproduction wrought iron or elegant wirework for a romantic Edwardian-style garden, or wooden steamer chairs for an authentic 1930s period piece.

Try not to be too swayed by the look of furniture. If you want to really relax properly, the seat has got to be comfortable. Cushions can make all the difference to an unyielding wooden or metal chair and removable fabric-covered foam pads are a must for built-in wooden benches. An abundance of cushions and rich fabrics also helps to create an impression of comfort and luxury for your outdoor 'room' and

fabric colours and patterns can further strengthen the overall design.

In most climates, if the furniture is to be left outside, it should be weather resistant. Metal furniture can rust if not properly coated and leave stains on the paving. Plastic furniture is lightweight and available in increasingly sophisticated designs and colours. It wipes clean easily and needs no maintenance, though it will eventually degrade in strong sunlight. Hardwood chairs and tables are attractive and long-lasting but are heavy and can be rather expensive. Softwood needs regular preservative treatment to prevent rotting, but is a cheaper option.

If there's room, a softwood picnic-table with integrated bench seats could be a practical option for family dining. Collapsible wooden framed chairs with

left: *Furniture as ornament.*

right: *A striking chair or bench seat set in a prominent position can have a tremendous visual impact.*

canvas seats, such as director's chairs, are inexpensive, comfortable enough to lounge in, light enough to move around easily and can be packed flat when not in use. They are ideal where space is limited. Hammocks are great for stretching out in and can be unhooked and rolled up when not in use.

And finally, if you'd rather allocate space and funds to plants rather than furniture, a simple bench made from a piece of reclaimed timber set on bricks will double as a plant display stand and an old wooden kitchen chair can be given a new lease of life with a bright coat of paint!

LIGHTING

Illuminating your garden serves two purposes. The first and most obvious is that it allows you to use the garden at night. The second is that you can still enjoy the garden from indoors when it's too cold to be outside. If your living room is separated from the garden by glass doors, then lighting the garden at night will visually extend the room

outdoors, making it seem larger than it really is.

Lighting can be as functional or as creative as you like. Once you've attended to essential areas such as

doorways, steps and any other changes in level, you can experiment with different lighting effects to suit the mood and setting. At night, the garden can be made to look utterly different to

Garden sculpture comes in many different forms as this delightful ceramic feature shows.

and texture such as *Fatsia japonica*, grasses, palms and yuccas. By lighting from the front or slightly to one side, you can throw strong leaf silhouettes on to the wall behind, with the effect of making the plants appear larger and more numerous.

Individual mini-spots which can be angled in any direction are useful for highlighting the structure of pergolas, trellis screens or archways or to pick out individual plants or garden ornaments below. When dining outside with friends or if you're having a party, garden candles and decorative lamps (oil or candle-powered) add greatly to the atmosphere and tiny white fairy lights create a magical effect when spiralled round pillars, woven through greenery or strung beneath a tent-like fabric canopy.

ORNAMENTS

Ornaments add the finishing touch to any garden and help to personalize the area and make it feel more lived in. Unfortunately, the choice of ornaments available from garden centres tends to be quite limited. A much greater range can be had from mail-order firms who

how it appears during the day. And in the darkness, colour becomes far less important than shape and texture. Most of the time we think of lights shining down on objects and surfaces, but in the garden, up-lighting can be subtle or dramatic without the unpleasant glare that downward-facing spotlights can create.

Some types of light can be set into the floor, flush with the surface, making it easy to see where you are stepping. With decking, this type of lighting is much easier to install

because of the gap below. Low-level lights also come fitted into the top of short columns or mushroom-topped pillars which cast a gentle light in all directions. Directional spotlights are used to create dramatic effects. A piece of statuary, a water-spouting wall mask or an ornate pot on a pedestal would be thrown into sharp relief by up-lighting from the front or to one side. Experiment to find the best angle for the light before fixing it in place. Plants also benefit greatly from this treatment, particularly ones with interesting shape

advertise in magazines for the home and garden. Some pieces can be quite expensive so before you buy, it's worth establishing if your chosen piece can be displayed properly. Also, ensure that it is genuinely weatherproof!

Site is very important and a well placed ornament can really draw the eye making a strong focal point. The term 'garden ornament' covers a great deal more than just traditional neo-classical styled figures and animals. Sculpture, for example, is made using many different materials, e.g. metal, glass, wood and wicker, as well as different styles. Other objects can also be used as garden ornaments. Fishing floats and large coloured glass carboys contrast beautifully with foliage plants and look well in more modern settings. Simple coloured glazed pots and ginger jars half-hidden amongst plants add an oriental note and shells, wave-carved pieces of driftwood, rocks and cobbles bring the sea to mind. Antique-style wirework birdcages and topiary frames suit romantic and period gardens and a group of stoneware flagons might be just the thing in a rustic, cottage garden setting.

Large statues, carved stone ornaments and giant Greek pithoi would weigh far too much for the average balcony or roof garden, but you can buy convincing reproductions in lightweight fibreglass.

WATER FEATURES

Because of the restrictions on weight for balconies and roof gardens, it's unlikely that any body of water is going to be very large. A raised pool lined with a shallow, fibreglass liner or butyl rubber lining cut to size is fairly easy to build and you could even make a staggered feature with water circulating from a higher to a lower pool. Use black-coloured liners for maximum reflection and to help disguise the fact that the water is not very deep. Try combining a water feature like this with planters full of lush foliage plants and a seat so that you relax and imagine yourself faraway. A wooden half-barrel lined with a waterproof sealant could be turned into a small pond and provided the water didn't freeze, could even support a couple of goldfish and some aquatic plants.

Self-contained fountains and mini cascades with a small electric pump can be fitted in a wide range of sealed ornamental pots and containers. The circulation pipe and electric cable are easily concealed with plants and pebbles. Adjust the water flow to the correct level and check for leaks. Keep the water feature sheltered from strong winds to avoid water loss.

Wall-mounted features are ideal where space is limited. However, camouflaging pipes and wiring is more difficult. One way to do this is to surround the feature with decorative trellis so that everything can be hidden in the space behind.

As with all electrical jobs, call in a professional if you are in any doubt as to what to do.

Differently sized terracotta pitchers link together to form a series of water cascades.

Index

Bold numbers indicate Practicalities section

Photo Credits

1 Sarah Quill/Archivio Veneziana; 6 Jack Townsend/Insight; 7 Ron Sutherland/GPL; 9 EWA; 10 Zefa; 11 Lamontagne/GPL; 12 Andrew Lawson; 13 Andrew Lawson (designer: Dan Pearson); 15 EWA; 16 EWA; 17 EWA; 18 Ron Sutherland/GPL; 19 EWA; 20 Robert O'Dea; 20-21 John Glover (designer: Stephen Crisp); 21 EWA; 23 Robert O'Dea; 24 Clive Nichols; 25 Clive Nichols (designer Anthony Noel); 26 EWA; 27 Clive Nichols (designer Randle Siddeley); 28 John Heseltine; 29 EWA; 30 Geoffrey Frosh; 31 EWA; 32 John Glover; 33 Geoffrey Frosh; 34 Ron Sutherland/GPL (designer Duane Paul); 35 Eric Crichton; 36 Clive Nichols (designer Anthony Noel); 37 Clive Nichols; 38 Robert O'Dea; 39 Clive Nichols (designer: Christian Wright); 40 S & O Mathews; 41 Clive Nichols; 42 Linda Burgess/GPL; 44 Clive Nichols; 45 Andrew Lawson; 46 Eric Crichton; 47 J S Sira/GPL; 48 Jack Townsend/Insight; 49 Steven Wooster/GPL (designer Anthony Paul); 50 Clive Nichols (designer Christopher Bradley-Hole); 51 Clive Nichols; 52 John Glover; 53 Eric Crichton; 54 Hugh Palmer; 55 Clive Nichols (designer Anthony Paul); 56 Linda Burgess/GPL; 57 Simon McBride/Comstock; 58 EWA; 59 Jacqui Hurst; 60 Michelle Garrett/Insight; 61 Wildlife Matters; 62 Clive Nichols; 63 Jenny Hendy; 64 Edifice/Nabarro; 65 Wildlife Matters; 66 John Glove/GPL; 67 Wildlife Matters; 68 Insight; 69 Photos Horticultural; 70 Lars Hallen; 71 John Glover (designer Stephen Crisp); 72 EWA; 73 (left) EWA; 73 (right) EWA; 75 Andrew Lawson (designer Dan Pearson); 76 Clive Nichols; 77 EWA; 78 Jack Townsend/Insight; 79 Michael Busselle; 80 Robert O'Dea; 81 Robert O'Dea; 83 Robert O'Dea; 83 EWA; 84 Michael Busselle; 84-85 C Thistlethwaite/Comstock; 85 Robert O'Dea; 86 Steven Wooster/GPL; 87 EWA; 88 Edifice/Lewis; 89 Nigel Temple/GPL; 90 EWA; 91 EWA; 92 EWA; 93 Wildlife Matters; 95 EWA; 96 Simon McBride; 97 Robert O'Dea; 99 Simon McBride; 100 (left) M J Keilty/Cephas; 100 (right) Sims; 101 Jack Townsend/Insight; 103 (left) Edifice/Lewis; 107 (left) Natural Image/Liz Gibbons; 118-119 John Heseltine; 119 Clive Nichols; 121 Clive Nichols (designer Randle Siddeley); 123 EWA; 124 Andrew Lawson; 125 EWA; 126 Clive Nichols (designer Vic Shanley); 127 Jack Townsend/Insight.

First published in 1997 by New Holland (Publishers) Ltd
London • Cape Town • Sydney • Singapore

24 Nutford Place
London W1H 6DQ
UK

P.O. Box 1144
Cape Town 8000
South Africa

3/2 Aquatic Drive
Frenchs Forest, NSW 2086
Australia

ISBN 1 85368 680 8

Designer: Grahame Dudley
Editor: Gillian Haslam
Editorial Direction: Yvonne McFarlane

Reproduction by Hirt and Carter (Pty) Ltd
Printed and bound in Singapore by Tien Wah Press Ltd